W9-ABU-972

LA COMUNIDAD
THE COMMUNITY

This book provides bilingual materials to teach a fun and comprehensive unit on the COMMUNITY. Included is a teacher's instruction section with details for each project along with ideas to use throughout the classroom. Discover the COMMUNITY using skills in reading, math, and spelling. Both Spanish and English versions of each project are included in one book!

Cover Photos:

Photo www.comstock.com

© 2005, Carson-Dellosa Publishing Company, Inc., Greensboro, North Carolina 27425. The purchase of this material entitles the buyer to reproduce worksheets and activities for classroom use only—not for commercial resale. Reproduction of these materials for an entire school or district is prohibited. No part of this book may be reproduced (except as noted above), stored in a retrieval system, or transmitted in any form or by any means (mechanically, electronically, recording, etc.) without the prior written consent of Carson-Dellosa Publishing Co., Inc.

Printed in the USA • All rights reserved.

ISBN 1-59441-424-6

Dear Family Letter (pages 6-7)

Dear Family,

We are starting a unit on the community. We will learn about people, places, and vehicles relating to our community. Please join us by including discussions about our community at home. Family discussions will help reinforce the concepts we are learning in class!

Sincerely,

Send this note home with students to let families know what is happening in the classroom. The letter introduces families to the upcoming unit on community.

My Community Certificate (pages 8-9)

This is a great way to recognize and reward students as they progress through the COMMUNITY unit.

Use the Community Workers Certificate as a specific incentive when students finish a defined list of projects or as a general award when the unit is complete. The certificates make a great classroom bulletin board display and provide students with take-home diplomas that they can be proud of.

Copy the certificates onto colorful paper or let students color their own certificates as a classroom art project.

Community Cards (pages 11-19)

The community cards included in this book can be used in a variety of ways to create fun and interesting learning flash cards.

FLASH CARDS

Make different flash card decks of varying degrees of difficulty to use as assessment tools. Display transparencies of the cards for reference during classroom discussions.

ASSEMBLY INSTRUCTIONS

Copy the desired community cards onto colorful paper or card stock and cut out. Copy the English cards on one side and copy the Spanish cards on the other side. Laminate cards for permanent use in the classroom or make sets for each student for a take-home project.

CONCENTRATION

(using word cards and community worker, community building, and community vehicle picture cards)

This ever-popular game helps children develop memory and matching skills. Concentration works best when played in small groups.

There are several variations of "Community Concentration": Younger students can match picture cards to the same picture cards. Increase difficulty by mixing and matching combinations. For example, students can match community worker picture cards to community vehicle picture cards.

Police

ASSEMBLY INSTRUCTIONS

Copy the desired community cards onto construction paper or card stock and cut out. Laminate cards for permanent use.

HOW TO PLAY

1. Mix up cards and place them upside down in rows.
2. Have students take turns choosing two cards at a time. If a student chooses two cards that match, she takes another turn. If there is no match, the next player takes a turn. The player with the most matched pairs wins the game!

Community Mobiles (pages 20-23)

This fun art project reinforces the skills and vocabulary in the COMMUNITY unit. Use it as a classroom decoration or to identify centers that focus on specific community groups. There are three community mobiles to make: Workers, Places, and Vehicles.

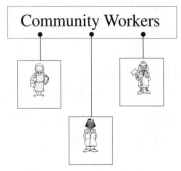

ASSEMBLY INSTRUCTIONS

Select a "header card" and desired community cards for a mobile and copy onto sturdy paper. Provide crayons, paint, or markers and have students color their mobile pieces. After coloring, have students fold and punch holes as indicated. Let them tape string, yarn, fishing line, or dental floss to the backs of the word cards. Then, have them glue the coordinating picture card on the back of each word card. When the glue dries, let them tie the community cards to the header cards. Hang the mobiles from the ceiling or a wall.

My Community Books (pages 24-31)

Students can create and color their own "My Community" books about people, places, and things in their community. Teachers can design a theme by choosing various covers and pages.

ASSEMBLY INSTRUCTIONS

Copy one book for each student. Copy cover pages onto sturdy paper and copy inside pages onto regular paper. Assemble and bind books using brass fasteners or staples.

Students can write stories or facts about community workers, places, and vehicles in their community books. Have students share their finished books with the class.

These books make a great take-home project. Have students complete several books to create their own "My Community" libraries! Finished books also make an excellent bulletin board display.

Bulletin Board Ideas

- Enlarge the strips (page 10) to make community bulletin board borders. Create borders for specific community themes such as a "career" board or "community vehicles" board. Have students color the pictures on the strips.

- Make a story starter board using community picture cards (pages 11-13). On sentence strips, write story starters about community workers, places, and vehicles. Leave a $4^1/4"$ x $3^3/8"$ blank space for each word or phrase that can be represented by a card. Glue the appropriate picture card to each strip. Display the strips on a bulletin board. Some suggested story starters include: "I met a grocer who juggled fruit . . ." and "I once saw a purple fire truck . . . ."

Estimados padres,

En la clase comenzamos un tema sobre la comunidad. Estamos aprendiendo sobre las personas, los lugares y los vehículos relacionados con nuestra comunidad.

Necesitamos su apoyo en la casa, incluyendo conversaciones sobre la comunidad. Las conversaciones familiares ayudarán a fortalecer los conceptos que se aprenden en clase.

Atentamente,

© Carson-Dellosa • La Comunidad • FI-704004

Dear Family,

We are starting a unit on the community. We will learn about people, places, and vehicles relating to our community.

Please join us by including discussions about our community at home. Family discussions will help reinforce the concepts we are learning in class!

Sincerely,

Mi comunidad

CERTIFICADO

Nombre: _____

¡Yo sé acerca de MI COMUNIDAD!

¡Felicidades!
Has aprendido sobre las personas, los lugares y los vehículos de la comunidad.

© Carson-Dellosa • La Comunidad • FI-704004

My Community

CERTIFICATE

I Know About MY COMMUNITY!

Name: _____

Congratulations! You have learned about community people, places, and vehicles!

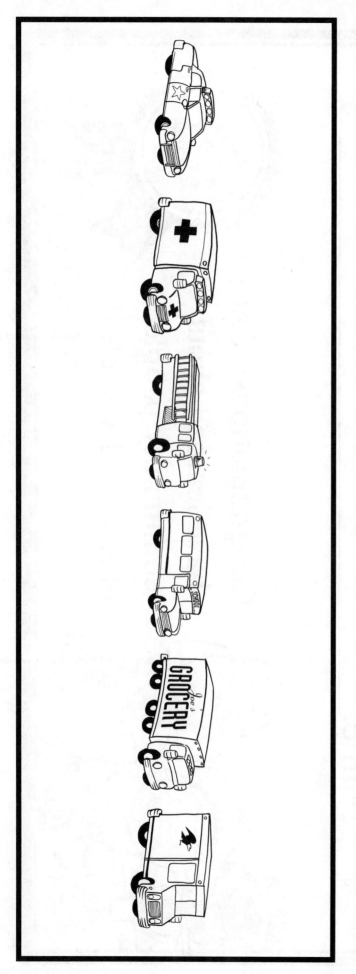

© Carson-Dellosa • La Comunidad • The Community • FI-704004

© Carson-Dellosa

© Carson-Dellosa

© Carson-Dellosa

bombero	doctor(a)
cartero	policía
abarrotero	maestro(a)

© Carson-Dellosa

doctor	firefighter
police officer	mail carrier
teacher	grocer

© Carson-Dellosa

estación de bomberos	hospital
oficina de correos	comisaría de policía
mercado	escuela

© Carson-Dellosa

hospital	fire station
police station	post office
school	grocery store

© Carson-Dellosa

camión de bomberos	ambulancia
camión de correos	patrulla
camión de víveres	transporte escolar

© Carson-Dellosa

ambulance	fire truck
police car	mail truck
school bus	grocery truck

© Carson-Dellosa

Móviles de la comunidad
Trabajadores, lugares y vehículos

Trabajadores de la comunidad

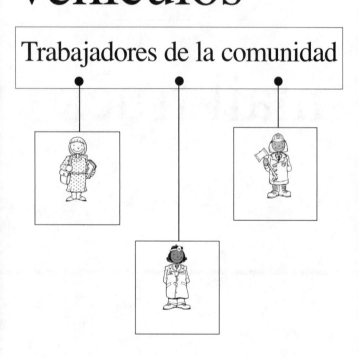

Trabajadores de la comunidad

Trabajadores de la comunidad

© Carson-Dellosa

Community Mobiles

Workers, Places, and Vehicles

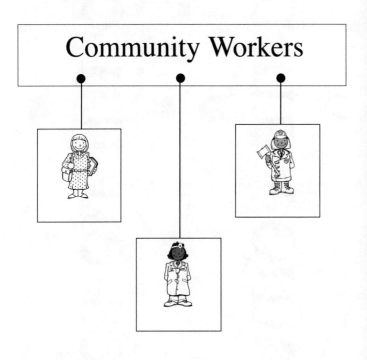

Community Workers

Community Workers

Community Workers

© Carson-Dellosa

Lugares en mi comunidad

Lugares en mi comunidad

Lugares en mi comunidad

Lugares en mi comunidad

Vehículos de la comunidad

Vehículos de la comunidad

Vehículos de la comunidad

Vehículos de la comunidad

© Carson-Dellosa

Community Vehicles

Community Vehicles

Places in My Community

Places in My Community

Trabajadores de la comunidad

Este libro fue hecho por:

_____

Nombre: _____

© Carson-Dellosa • La Comunidad • FI-704004

Community Workers

This Book Was

Created By:

Name: _____

Lugares de la comunidad

Este libro fue hecho por:

Nombre: _____

© Carson-Dellosa • La Comunidad • FI-704004

Community Places

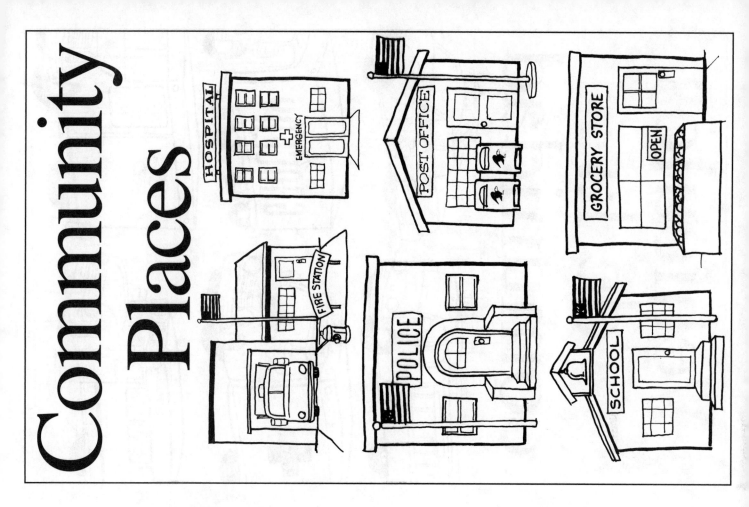

This Book Was
Created By:

Name: _____

Vehículos de la comunidad

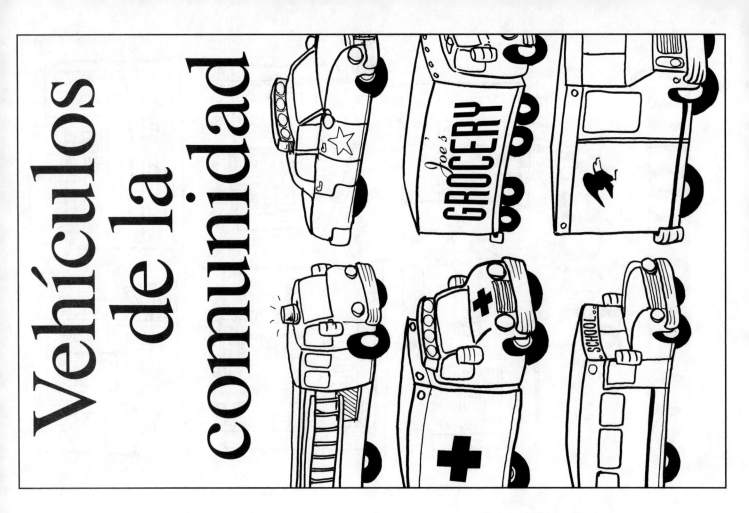

Este libro fue hecho por:

Nombre: _____

© Carson-Dellosa • La Comunidad • FI-704004

Community Vehicles

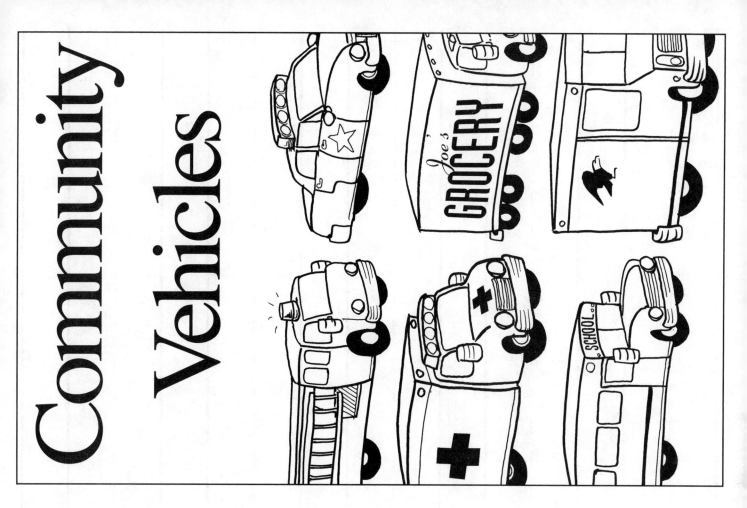

This Book Was
Created By:

Name: _____

© Carson-Dellosa • The Community • FI-704004

© Carson-Dellosa • La Comunidad • FI-704004

© Carson-Dellosa • The Community • FI-704004

Nombre:_____

Conjunto de la comunidad

Une el trabajador y el vehículo correcto con una línea.

© Carson-Dellosa • La Comunidad • FI-704004

Community Match

Draw a line from each worker to the correct community vehicle.

© Carson-Dellosa • The Community • FI-704004

Nombre:_____

Círculo de la comunidad

Haz un círculo alrededor del nombre correcto de cada edificio.

comisaría de policía
hospital

escuela
estación de bomberos

mercado
comisaría de policía

oficina de correos
comisaría de policía

escuela
estación de bomberos

oficina de correos
hospital

© Carson-Dellosa • La Comunidad • FI-704004

Name: _____

Community Circle

Circle the correct name of each building.

police station
hospital

school
fire station

grocery store
police station

post office
police station

school
fire station

post office
hospital

© Carson-Dellosa • The Community • FI-704004

Nombre: _____

Círculo de la comunidad

Haz un círculo alrededor del nombre correcto de cada trabajador.

doctora

maestra

abarrotero

bombero

cartero

policía

policía

doctor

bombero

maestra

abarrotero

cartero

© Carson-Dellosa • La Comunidad • FI-704004

Name:_____

Community Circle

Circle the correct name
of each worker.

doctor
teacher

grocer
firefighter

mail carrier
police officer

police officer
doctor

firefighter
teacher

grocer
mail carrier

© Carson-Dellosa • The Community • FI-704004

Círculo de la comunidad

Haz un círculo alrededor del nombre correcto de cada vehículo.

patrulla

camión de bomberos

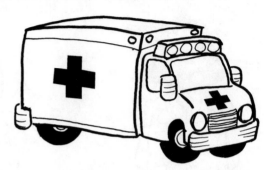

transporte escolar

ambulancia

camión de víveres

ambulancia

transporte escolar

patrulla

camión de correos

camión de bomberos

patrulla

camión de correos

© Carson-Dellosa • La Comunidad • FI-704004

Name: _____

Community Circle

Circle the correct name of each vehicle.

police car
fire truck

school bus
ambulance

grocery truck
ambulance

school bus
police car

mail truck
fire truck

police car
mail truck

© Carson-Dellosa • The Community • FI-704004

Nombre:_____

Llena los espacios

Escribe la letra que falta en cada palabra.

 __olicía

__arta

 __amión de bomberos

__ibros

 __laca

__ransporte escolar

 __amión de __íveres

__scuela

 __amión de __orreos

__barrotero

  © Carson-Dellosa • La Comunidad • FI-704004

Fill in the Blanks

Fill in the missing letter in each word.

 __olice officer

__etter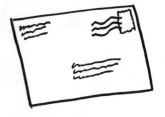

 __ire __ruck

__ooks

 __adge

__chool __us

 __rocery __ruck

__chool

 __ail __ruck

__rocer

Llena los espacios

Escribe la letra que falta en cada palabra.

ambulanci___

oficina de correo___

maestr___

escuel___

policí___

vívere___

bomber___

cart___

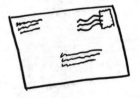

plac___

hospita___

© Carson-Dellosa • La Comunidad • FI-704004

Name:_____

Fill in the Blanks

Fill in the missing letter in each word.

 ambulanc___

post offic___

 teache___

schoo___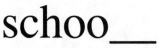

 polic___ officer

grocerie___

 firefighte___

lette___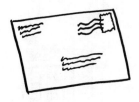

 badg___

hospita___

© Carson-Dellosa • The Community • FI-704004

Llena los espacios

Escribe la letra que falta en cada palabra.

do__tora

bombe__o

merca__o

boca de ag__a

estet__scopio

pla__a

v__veres

carte__o

hos__ital

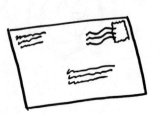

car__a

© Carson-Dellosa • La Comunidad • FI-704004

Name:_____

Fill in the Blanks

Fill in the missing letter in each word.

do__tor

firefigh__er

groc__ry store

fire h__drant

stet__oscope

bad__e

g__oceries

mail ca__rier

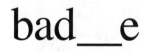

hos__ital

lett__r

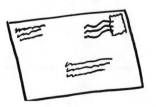

Nombre:_____

Deletreo de la comunidad

Escribe el nombre
de cada trabajador.

_____

_____

© Carson-Dellosa • La Comunidad • FI-704004

Name: _____

Community Spell

Write the name
of each worker.

_____ _____ _____

_____ _____ _____

Nombre:_____

Deletrea correctamente

Haz un círculo alrededor de la palabra correcta de cada grupo.

doktr
doctora
poctor

oficina de correos
officino de correas
oficina de koreos

abarrotero
aborotero
aborrotoro

ospital
hospital
hospetall

cartero
cartiro
carterro

estación de boleros
estación de bomberos
estación de boberos

polizia
policia
policía

mercado
merkado
mercato

bomero
bombero
bomber

masttra
mastra
maestra

© Carson-Dellosa • La Comunidad • FI-704004

Name:_____

Spell It Right

Circle the word that is spelled correctly in each group.

doktr
doctor
poctor

post office
pos afese
post ofece

grocer
growser
greozer

ospital
hospital
hospetall

mail carrier
male carrier
mail carryer

feir station
fire station
fire stashon

poliz officer
polise osifer
police officer

grocery store
grocerie store
grocery stoor

fier fighter
firefighter
fire fiter

techr
teecheer
teacher

Nombre:_____

Deletrea correctamente

Haz un círculo alrededor de la palabra correcta de cada grupo.

bombero
dombero
pombero

transporta esular
transporte escolar
trensporte escoolar

doctora
loctora
zoctora

camión de bomberos
camión de dombero
camión de pombero

bolicía
folicía
policía

emblulancia
ombulancia
ambulancia

caestra
maestra
faestra

camión de correos
kamión de correo
damión de correo

kartero
gartero
cartero

patrulla
datrulla
batrulla

  © Carson-Dellosa • La Comunidad • FI-704004

Name:_____

Spell It Right

fire fiter
tire fighter
firefighter

lchool bus
school bus
tchool bus

doctor
loctor
zoctor

fire truck
yire truck
qire truck

bolice officer
police osifer
police officer

embulance
ombulance
ambulance

ceacher
teacher
feacher

jail truck
mail truck
sail truck

mail carier
pail carrier
mail carrier

police car
solice car
volice car

© Carson-Dellosa • The Community • FI-704004

Deletreo de la comunidad

Escribe el nombre de cada vehículo.

© Carson-Dellosa • La Comunidad • FI-704004

Name:_____

Community Spell

Write the name of each type of vehicle.

_____

_____

_____

_____

_____

_____

© Carson-Dellosa • The Community • FI-704004

Nombre:_____

Deletreo de la comunidad

Escribe el nombre de cada lugar de la comunidad.

_____

_____

_____

_____

© Carson-Dellosa • La Comunidad • FI-704004

Name:_____

Community Spell

Write the name of each type of community place.

_____

_____

_____

_____

Colorea las palabras

Lee el cuento.
Responde a cada pregunta.

Las escuelas son lugares de la comunidad donde la gente va para aprender a leer, escribir y deletrear. Los maestros y las maestras también nos ayudan a aprender matemáticas y ciencias. Los estudiantes mayores van a escuelas especiales para aprender a ser doctores, maestros y bomberos. Algunos estudiantes llegan a la escuela en transporte escolar. Los autobuses pueden llevar a la gente al otro lado de la ciudad o a otras ciudades.

Busca en el cuento la palabra "las." Cada vez que encuentres la palabra "las" coloréala de amarillo.

1. ¿Cuántas veces encontraste la palabra "las" en el cuento?

_____

Usa un creyón verde y colorea todas las palabras "escuelas."

2. ¿Cuántas veces encontraste la palabra "escuelas"?

_____

 © Carson-Dellosa • La Comunidad • FI-704004

Name:_____

Color the Words

Read the story below.
Answer the questions.

Schools are places in our community where we go to learn to read, write, and spell. Teachers also help us to learn math and science. Older students go to special schools where they learn to be doctors, teachers, and firefighters. Some children ride to school on a school bus. Buses can take people to the other side of their town or even to different cities.

Look in the story and find all of the times the word "to" is used and color it yellow.

1. How many times did you find and color the word "to"?

_____

Use a green crayon and color the words "school" and "schools" each time they are used.

2. How many times did you find "school" or "schools"?

_____

Nombre:_____

Colorea las palabras

Lee el cuento.
Responde a cada pregunta.

El cartero lleva las cartas y los paquetes al buzón de tu casa. Los carteros y las carteras trabajan en las oficinas de correos. Puedes comprar sellos y enviar cartas y paquetes en la oficina de correos. Los carteros y las carteras clasifican el correo por vecindarios. Ellos usan camiones de correos para entregar las cartas y los paquetes.

Busca en el cuento las palabras que comienzan con la letra "c" y coloréalas de azul.

1. ¿Cuántas palabras encontraste que comienzan con la letra "c"?

   _____

Usa un creyón rojo y colorea las palabras que comienzan con la letra "l."

2. ¿Cuántas veces encontraste palabras que comienzan con la letra "l"? _____

  © Carson-Dellosa • La Comunidad • FI-704004

Name:_____

Color the Words

A mail carrier takes letters and packages to the mailbox at your house. Mail carriers work at post offices. You can buy stamps and mail letters and packages at a post office. Mail carriers sort the mail according to neighborhoods. They use mail trucks to deliver the letters and packages.

Look in the story and find all of the times the letter "m" is used at the beginning of a word and circle it in blue.

1. How many times did you find and color words that begin with the letter "m"?_____

Use a red crayon and color all of the words that begin with "s."

2. How many times did you find and color the letter "s" at the beginning of a word?_____

Nombre:_____

Colorea las palabras

Lee el cuento.
Responde a cada pregunta.

Los policías manejan patrullas. Algunos
policías montan en bicicleta y a caballo.
Trabajan en las comisarías de policía y en la
comunidad. Ellos hasta vienen a nuestras
escuelas a enseñarnos. Ellos nos ayudan a
mantener la comunidad segura. Ellos quieren
que la gente siga las reglas de nuestra
comunidad. Los policías llevan uniformes
y sombreros especiales. Si necesitas ayuda
siempre pregúntale a un policía.

Busca en el cuento las palabras que llevan acento o tilde y coloréalas
en rojo.

1. ¿Cuántas veces encontraste palabras que llevan acento o tilde?

   _____

Usa un creyón marrón y colorea todas las palabras que terminan
con una "s."

2. ¿Cuántas veces encontraste palabras que terminan con la
   letra "s"? _____

                                   © Carson-Dellosa • La Comunidad • FI-704004

Name:_____

Color the Words

Police officers drive police cars. Some police officers ride bikes and horses. They work at police stations and in the community. Police officers even come to our schools to teach us. They help keep our communities safe by making sure people obey our laws and rules. Police officers wear special uniforms and hats. If you need help, you can always ask a police officer.

Look in the story and color each word that begins with a vowel red.

1. How many times did you find and color words that begin with vowels?_____

Use a brown crayon and color all of the words that end with "s."

2. How many times did you find words that end in the letter "s"?

_____

Nombre:_____

Llena los espacios

Usa las palabras de abajo para completar cada oración.

1. El _____ trabaja en la comisaría de policía.

2. Mi padre es un cartero. Él maneja un _____
   _____.

3. Mi maestra nunca llega tarde a la _____.

4. Un bombero conecta la manguera a la _____
   _____.

5. Compramos nuestra comida en el _____.

6. El policía usa una _____ .

7. La _____ lleva a las personas al
   hospital rápidamente.

8. Nuestro _____ nos lleva a la
   escuela cada día.

9. Fui a la _____ para mandar
   una carta.

10. Vimos un _____ en frente de la
    estación de bomberos.

Palabras:
oficina de correos   transporte escolar   escuela   policía
camión de correos   boca de agua   placa   mercado
camión de bomberos   ambulancia

   © Carson-Dellosa • La Comunidad • FI-704004

Name:_____

Use the word bank below to complete each sentence.

1. The _____ works at the police station.
2. My father is a mail carrier. He drives a _____
   _____ .
3. My teacher is never late for _____ .
4. A firefighter connects the fire hose to a _____
   _____ .
5. We buy our food at the _____ .
6. A _____ is worn by a police officer.
7. An _____ takes people to the
   hospital in a hurry.
8. The _____ takes us to school each day.
9. I went to the _____ to mail a letter.
10. We saw a _____ in front of the
    fire station.

Word Bank:

mail truck	police officer	grocery store
school	badge	post office
school bus	fire truck	ambulance
fire hydrant		

Nombre:_____

Cuenta los trabajadores

Haz un círculo alrededor de la cantidad correcta.

¿Cuántas maestras?   5   7

¿Cuántas doctoras?   4   6

¿Cuántos carteros?   8   10

¿Cuántos bomberos?   6   10

¿Cuántos policías?   5   7

¿Cuántos abarroteros?   10   9

© Carson-Dellosa • La Comunidad • FI-704004

Name: _____

Count the Workers

Circle the correct amount.

How many teachers?   5   7

How many doctors?   4   6

How many mail carriers?   8   10

How many firefighters?   6   10

How many police officers?   5   7

How many grocers?   10   9

© Carson-Dellosa • The Community • FI-704004   65

Nombre:_____

Cuenta los edificios

Haz un círculo alrededor de la cantidad correcta.

¿Cuántas escuelas?   2   3

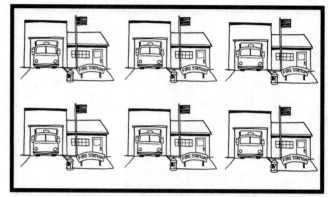

¿Cuántas estaciones de bomberos?   4   6

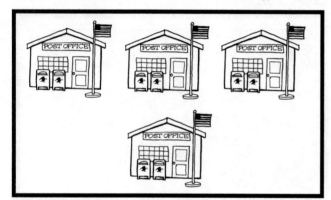

¿Cuántas oficinas de correos?   4   5

¿Cuántas comisarías de policía?   5   8

¿Cuántos hospitales?   8   9

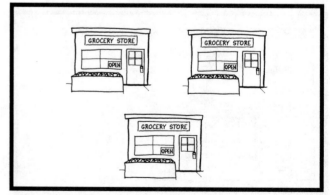

¿Cuántos mercados?   3   6

© Carson-Dellosa • La Comunidad • FI-704004

Name:_____

Count the Buildings

Circle the correct amount.

How many schools?   2   3

How many fire stations?   4   6

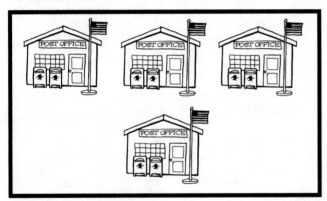

How many post offices?   4   5

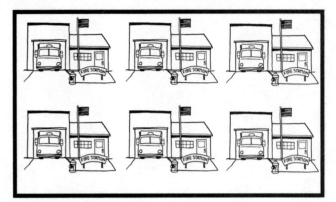

How many police stations?   5   8

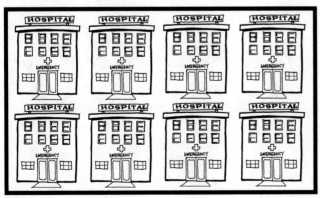

How many hospitals?   8   9

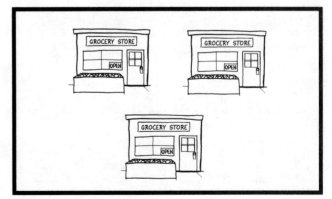

How many grocery stores?   3   6

Cuenta los vehículos

Haz un círculo alrededor de la cantidad correcta.

¿Cuántos transportes escolar? 7 9

¿Cuántos camiones de correos? 9 10

¿Cuántas ambulancias? 10 12

¿Cuántos camiones de bomberos? 4 8

¿Cuántas patrullas? 6 9

¿Cuántos camiones de víveres? 10 9

© Carson-Dellosa • La Comunidad • FI-704004

Count the Vehicles

Circle the
correct amount.

How many
school buses?   7   9

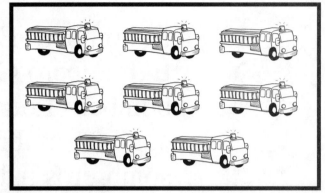

How many
fire trucks?   4   8

How many
mail trucks?   9   10

How many
police cars?   6   9

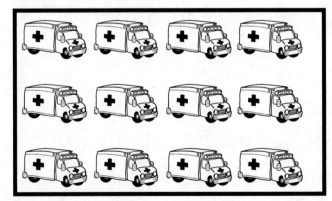

How many
ambulances?   10   12

How many
grocery trucks?   10   9

Problemas de matemáticas

Resuelve cada problema y muestra tu trabajo.

El bombero Eduardo tenía 3 sombreros. El bombero Carlos tenía 6 sombreros. El bombero Eduardo puso sus sombreros con los sombreros de Carlos. ¿Cuántos sombreros había en total?

La doctora Julia examinó a 4 pacientes antes del almuerzo y 5 pacientes después del almuerzo. ¿Cuántos pacientes examinó después del almuerzo?

El policía Sam salió de la comisaría de policía a las nueve. El manejó por media hora; luego paró y recogió al policía Tomás. ¿A qué hora recogió al policía Tomás?

La maestra Teresa enseña música 4 horas cada día. Ella también enseña educación física 2 horas al día. ¿Cuántas horas enseña cada día la maestra Teresa?

© Carson-Dellosa • La Comunidad • FI-704004

Community Story Problems

Complete each problem and show your work.

Bill had 3 fire hats. Carl had 6 fire hats. Bill put his fire hats with Carl's fire hats. How many hats did the firefighters have all together?

Doctor Joyce saw 4 patients before lunch and 5 patients after lunch. How many patients did Doctor Joyce see after she ate lunch?

Police Officer Sam left the police station at 9:00. He drove for half an hour then stopped and picked up Police Officer Tom. What time did he pick up Police Officer Tom?

Ms. Parks teaches music 4 hours each day. She teaches PE for 2 hours. How many hours each day does Ms. Parks teach?

Nombre:_____

Problemas de matemáticas
Resuelve cada problema y muestra tu trabajo.

 Ocho bomberos fueron rápidamente al incendio. Después de una hora el fuego fue controlado y todos los bomberos salieron menos 3. ¿Cuántos bomberos regresaron a la estación de bomberos?

 La doctora vino a la escuela y examinó a 47 estudiantes antes del almuerzo. Después de comer estaba cansada y examinó solamente a 32 estudiantes más. ¿Cuántos estudiantes examinó la doctora durante todo el día?

 Normalmente el policía va a la comisaría de policía 25 días cada mes. En enero el policía estuvo enfermo 3 días y faltó 4 días más cuando fue a la escuela para enseñar clases. ¿Cuántos días fue el policía a la estación durante el mes de enero?

 La maestra Teresa tiene 32 estudiantes en su clase. Hoy 2 estudiantes estuvieron ausentes y otros 6 fueron a una excursión para los miembros de la banda. ¿Cuántos estudiantes tuvo la maestra Teresa en su clase hoy?

© Carson-Dellosa • La Comunidad • FI-704004

Name:_____

Community Story Problems

Eight firefighters rushed to a fire. After an hour, the fire was under control so all but 3 firefighters left. How many firefighters left to go back to the fire station?

The doctor came to school and saw 47 students before lunch. After lunch, the doctor was tired and only saw 32 more students. How many students did the doctor see all day?

The police officer normally goes to the police station 25 days each month. In January, he was sick 3 days and missed another 4 days when he was at school teaching classes. How many days did the police officer go to the station?

Ms. Terry has 32 students in her class. Today 2 students were absent and 6 students went on a special field trip for band members. How many students does Ms. Terry have in her class today?

Nombre:_____

Busca las palabras

¿Puedes encontrar las palabras escondidas?
Hicimos un círculo alrededor de "placa."
¿Puedes encontrar las demás palabras?

```
r  e  a  f  a  w  b  u  z  ó  n  e
n  s  b  m  y  q  f  d  b  x  b  n
a  c  a  e  x  c  a  r  t  a  x  a
w  u  r  r  m  a  e  s  t  r  o  r
s  e  r  c  k  r  x  s  o  v  e  x
m  l  o  a  a  a  m  r  m  d  v  m
p  a  t  d  e  v  e  v  j  o  y  s
l  m  e  o  h  b  g  c  e  c  j  a
a  o  r  o  m  i  f  r  q  t  o  x
c  b  o  o  o  a  z  o  o  o  k  e
a  l  b  k  f  u  l  i  b  r  o  s
n  w  f  t  r  g  p  r  z  o  l  c
```

placa   maestro   libros   buzón

mercado   escuela   bombero   carta

doctor   abarrotero

© Carson-Dellosa • La Comunidad • FI-704004

Word Find

Can you find the hidden words?
One word is circled for you. Find
the other words.

```
a  j  o  t  e  a  c  h  e  r  l  l
m  a  i  l  b  o  x  e  e  r  f  i
i  r  e  i  l  a  e  e  d  l  i  r
l  i  r  d  e  o  u  g  t  u  r  e
e  s  h  f  t  s  b  a  d  g  e  b
t  e  f  t  t  r  c  s  a  r  f  s
e  s  i  g  e  b  g  c  n  s  i  d
s  l  r  r  r  b  n  h  h  r  g  o
t  s  e  o  e  o  i  o  o  t  h  c
o  a  m  c  c  o  t  o  p  i  t  t
r  d  a  e  e  k  i  l  a  s  e  o
e  h  n  r  a  s  p  p  t  t  r  r
```

badge   teacher   books   mailbox
store   school   firefighter letter
doctor   grocer

© Carson-Dellosa • The Community • FI-704004

Nombre:_____

Busca las palabras

¿Puedes encontrar las palabras escondidas?
Hicimos un círculo alrededor de "ambulancia."
¿Puedes encontrar las demás palabras?

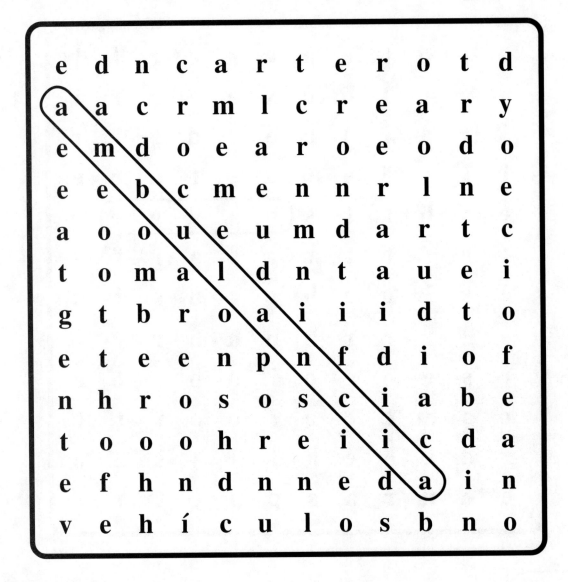

```
e  d  n  c  a  r  t  e  r  o  t  d
a  a  c  r  m  l  c  r  e  a  r  y
e  m  d  o  e  a  r  o  e  o  d  o
e  e  b  c  m  e  n  n  r  l  n  e
a  o  o  u  e  u  m  d  a  r  t  c
t  o  m  a  l  d  n  t  a  u  e  i
g  t  b  r  o  a  i  i  i  d  t  o
e  t  e  e  n  p  n  f  d  i  o  f
n  h  r  o  s  o  s  c  i  a  b  e
t  o  o  o  h  r  e  i  i  c  d  a
e  f  h  n  d  n  n  e  d  a  i  n
v  e  h  í  c  u  l  o  s  b  n  o
```

ambulancia   bombero   gente   correo
edificio   hospital   cartero vehículos
comunidad

© Carson-Dellosa • La Comunidad • FI-704004

Word Find

Can you find the hidden words?
One word is circled for you. Find the
other words.

```
g b p o s t o f f i c e
f m b e h y v v a f h g
q a u n o f a s m i v r
h i i y s p g a b r e o
l l l i p n l x u e h c
e c d d i l m e l t i e
z a i z t a c t a r c r
q r n v a u z t n u l i
a r g b l w j q c c e e
p i b y e d c i e k s s
w e c o m m u n i t y l
w r p o p t x d d e c j
```

ambulance   fire truck   mail carrier   people

building   groceries   post office   vehicles

community   hospital

© Carson-Dellosa • The Community • FI-704004

Answer Key

Pages 32-33

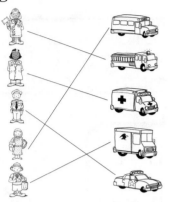

Page 34
from left to right and top to bottom: comisaría de policía, estación de bomberos, mercado, oficina de correos, escuela, hospital

Page 35
from left to right and top to bottom: police station, fire station, grocery store, post office, school, hospital

Page 36
from left to right and top to bottom: doctora, bombero, cartero, policía, maestra, abarrotero

Page 37
from left to right and top to bottom: doctor, firefighter, mail carrier, police officer, teacher, grocer

Page 38
from left to right and top to bottom: patrulla, ambulancia, camión de víveres, transporte escolar, camión de bomberos, camión de correos

Page 39
from left to right and top to bottom: police car, ambulance, grocery truck, school bus, fire truck, mail truck

Page 40
from top to bottom: policía, carta, camión de bomberos, libros, placa, transporte escolar, camión de víveres, escuela, camión de correos, abarrotero

Page 41
from top to bottom: police officer, letter, fire truck, books, badge, school bus, grocery truck, school, mail truck, grocer

Page 42
from top to bottom: ambulancia, oficina de correos, maestra, escuela, policía, víveres, bombero, carta, placa, hospital

Page 43
from top to bottom: ambulance, post office, teacher, school, police officer, groceries, firefighter, letter, badge, hospital

Page 44
from top to bottom: doctora, bombero, mercado, boca de agua, estetoscopio, placa, víveres, cartero, hospital, carta

Page 45
from top to bottom: doctor, firefighter, grocery store, fire hydrant, stethoscope, badge, groceries, mail carrier, hospital, letter

Page 46
from left to right and top to bottom: doctora, bombero, cartero, policía, maestra, abarrotero

Page 47
from left to right and top to bottom: doctor, firefighter, mail carrier, police officer, teacher, grocer

© Carson-Dellosa • La Comunidad • The Community • FI-704004

Answer Key

Page 48

from top to bottom and left to right: doctora, abarrotero, cartero, policía, bombero, oficina de correos, hospital, estacíon de bomberos, mercado, maestra

Page 49

from top to bottom and left to right: doctor, grocer, mail carrier, police officer, firefighter, post office, hospital, fire station, grocery store, teacher

Page 50

from top to bottom and left to right: bombero, doctora, policía, maestra, cartero, transporte escolar, camión de bomberos, ambulancia, camión de correos, patrulla

Page 51

from top to bottom and left to right: firefighter, doctor, police officer, teacher, mail carrier, school bus, fire truck, ambulance, mail truck, police car

Page 52

from top to bottom and left to right: patrulla, camión de víveres, camión de bomberos, ambulancia, transporte escolar, camión de correos

Page 53

from top to bottom and left to right: police car, grocery truck, fire truck, ambulance, school bus, mail truck

Page 54

from top to bottom and left to right: comisaría de policía, oficina de correos, estación de bomberos, escuela, mercado, hospital

Page 55

from top to bottom and left to right: police station, post office, fire station, school, grocery store, hospital

Page 56

1. 2 times, 2. 2 times

Page 57

1. 8 times, 2. 4 times

Page 58

1. 16 times, 2. 10 times

Page 59

1. 7 times, 2. 2 times

Page 60

1. 8 accents or tildes, 2. 22 times

Page 61

1. 20 times, 2. 16 times

Page 62

1. policía, 2. camión de correos, 3. escuela, 4. boca de agua, 5. mercado, 6. placa, 7. ambulancia, 8. transporte escolar, 9. oficina de correos, 10. camión de bomberos

Page 63

1. police officer, 2. mail truck, 3. school, 4. fire hydrant, 5. grocery store, 6. badge, 7. ambulance, 8. school bus, 9. post office, 10. fire truck

Pages 64-65

from top to bottom and left to right: 5, 8, 7, 6, 10, 9

Answer Key

Page 66-67

from top to bottom and left to right: 3, 4, 8, 6, 5, 3

Pages 68-69

from top to bottom and left to right: 7, 10, 12, 8, 6, 9

Page 70

9 sombreros, 5 pacientes, 9:30, 6 horas

Page 71

9 fire hats, 5 patients, 9:30, 6 hours

Page 72

5 bomberos, 79 estudiantes, 18 días, 24 estudiantes

Page 73

5 firefighters, 79 students, 18 days, 24 students

Page 74

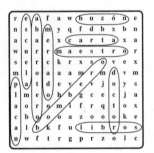

Page 75

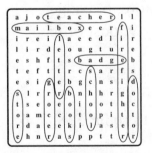

Page 76

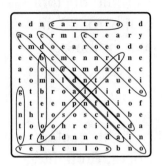

Page 77

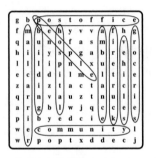

© Carson-Dellosa • La Comunidad • The Community • FI-704004